RSVP SOBER
Your Guided Journal for Socialising Alcohol-Free

RSVP SOBER
Your Guided Journal for Socialising Alcohol-Free

Copyright © 2023 by Rebecca Weller
All rights reserved.
Published by Mod By Dom Pty Ltd 2023
Perth, WA, Australia

No part of this publication may be reproduced, stored in a retrieval system, distributed, or transmitted in any form or by any means, including photocopying, recording, or other electronic or mechanical methods, without the prior written permission of the publisher or author, except in the case of brief quotations embodied in articles and reviews and certain other noncommercial uses permitted by copyright law.

The content of this book is for general information only. Each person's physical, emotional, and spiritual condition is unique. The content in this book is not intended to replace or interrupt the reader's relationship with a physician or other professional. Please consult your doctor or health professional for matters pertaining to your specific health concerns.

Cover and Interior Design by Dominic Garczynski.

Paperback ISBN: 9780645489521

ModByDom.com

RSVP SOBER
Your Guided Journal for Socialising Alcohol-Free

Rebecca Weller

Mod By Dom ~ Australia

This journal belongs to:

Contents

Welcome! — 9

Part 1: Setting the Stage — 13
- What if it's Actually Better? — 14
- Declutter your Calendar — 19
- Facebook Fantasyland — 27

Part 2: Prep like a Sober Rockstar — 33
- Boost Your Happy Vibes — 34
- Farewell, FOMO — 43

Part 3: Mindset Shifts — 51
- Magical Reframing — 52
- Setting Your Intentions — 59
- Fast Forward Game — 67

Part 4: Get this Party Started! — 77
- Perfect Playlist — 78
- The Power of Gratitude — 83
- Self Care Travel Kit — 86

Part 5: Confidence Hacks — 95

- Action Creates Confidence — 96
- Spot Your Exits — 100
- Frockin' Fabulous — 104
- Aromatic Anchoring — 109
- Introversion is my Superpower — 113

Part 6: Peer Pressure — 117

- Fitting Out — 118
- Owning It! — 124
- It's Not Me, It's You — 127
- Saying No — 136

Part 7: Rocking the Event — 143

- Sober is Sexy — 144
- Choosing Your Energy — 147
- The Curiosity Game — 153

Part 8: Looking Ahead — 161

- Morning After Reflection — 162
- Bumps in the Road — 172
- Metamorphosis — 175
- Shake up the Scene — 179

Final Love Note — 182

"Because in the end, it didn't matter whether I drank every day, or binge-drank once a week. What mattered was the effect drinking was having on my soul."

– *A Happier Hour*

Welcome!

I'm so thrilled you're here. Congratulations on choosing this book, and stepping into a whole new world of unshakeable confidence.

Scared of socialising sober? You're not alone.

Every single week, beautiful souls write to ask me, "Bex, what advice do you have for people who might be afraid to go to a party sober?"

And each time, my mind immediately flashes back to when I first decided to embark on my own sobriety odyssey.

I desperately wanted to be free of the binge drinking trap. To feel playful, with confidence that was authentically *me* - not poured from a bottle.

But I was terrified. It was all so new and nerve-wracking. I had no idea how to navigate social events without a drink in my hand. Not to mention the fact that I honestly believed sobriety meant never having fun *ever again*.

cue dramatic music Da-da-daaaaaa...

If you've just stopped drinking (or are about to), it's perfectly understandable to find yourself feeling extra nervous or raw with emotion right now. Early sobriety can be fun, exciting and magical. It can also be really freaking tough! It's a big lifestyle change that involves doing new things, and learning to *live* again in many ways. This stuff takes courage!

Buckle Up

Going to events sober can feel like one of the trickiest and most precarious parts of early sobriety. I'd rarely been to an event alcohol-free in over twenty years, so those first few invitations felt really intimidating.

But, like any skill, learning to socialise sober simply takes time and practice. After a while, it doesn't even bother you anymore *(promise!)*.

This guided journal will help you get there.

Each page is filled with deep, powerful questions designed to inspire change and help you feel safe as you explore a whole new way of being in the world.

We'll cover game-changing tips for preparing for events, including magical mindset shifts, mantras that can move mountains, and entirely practical strategies you can apply immediately.

From busting out of the pre-gaming habit, to all the delights that are mind-blowingly better (*helloooo*, hangover-free mornings!), I can't wait to share with you the savviest strategies to help you fall madly in love with alcohol-free socialising *(truly!)*.

Feel free to scribble outside the lines and dig deep as you design your very own action plan to help you feel empowered and excited as you head into your next party, function, BBQ, or... *dare I say it?* Even a wedding!

But first, a bonus tip.

Learning to love events when you're sober takes *time*.

Approaching each new soirée as a *science experiment* can help you maintain your sense of humour and avoid getting lost in the fear of change.

As we work through this journal together, whenever you find yourself feeling apprehensive, try repeating the mantra: **"This is an *experiment* – I want to see what sober socialising feels like."** Afterwards, record your 'lab notes' in this journal.

Become a curious observer, and approach this whole endeavour with child-like wonder. What did you love about parties when you were little? Delicious food; hilarious games; catching up with friends; having the chance to wear new clothes that make you happy?

Because we *know* what parties are like when we get boozy, right? We've had years – if not *decades* – of experience with that.

What we *don't* know is a social life free of the spectacle that comes with drinking – the hangovers, arguments, shame and regret.

Don't you want to see what happens?

What could that life look and feel like? What new activities or places could you discover? What epiphanies could you experience?

Grab your favourite pen, and let's find out…

Part 1:
Setting the Stage

"I'd always believed that alcohol helped me to relax and celebrate, but seriously, what was relaxing about constantly chasing more? What's to celebrate when a toxic substance holds you in such a vice-like grip?"

- A Happier Hour

WHAT IF IT'S ACTUALLY *BETTER?*

Let's kick off this party with an exploration into our old, worn-out beliefs versus the possibility of a very exciting new reality, shall we?

On Day 30 of my sobriety, I woke up barely believing I'd made it to that seemingly impossible milestone. That fateful day also happened to be my birthday; the day I turned 39.

That night, for the first time in my adult life, I celebrated my birthday sober.

Instead of my usual champagne and dancing-on-tables-with-a-hundred-friends celebration, my love Dominic and I had a chilled night in.

We made fajitas for dinner (my fave!), and shared some fancy chocolate. I filled my crystal goblet with sparkling mineral water and fresh lime, and we watched an '80s flick.

And despite my every belief, expectation and fear about how boring a sober birthday would feel, it actually felt really flippin' *good*.

As I went to bed that night, it floored me to realise that I'd actually loved celebrating it sober!

All those years I'd told myself I loved getting smashed and whooping it up on my birthday, and it turns out I actually... *didn't*. I'd simply never given myself a chance to find that out before.

THIS WASN'T A ONCE-OFF

It happened many times as I made my way through a year of sober firsts. First sober trip, Summer, Christmas, New Years, Valentines Day... *all* events I was terrified about experiencing sober - were actually *better* without the booze.

It blew my mind.

Looking back, if someone had asked me why I was afraid to go to an event sober, I would have said, "Because it'll be boring if I don't drink."

I'd never stopped to consider the bigger questions, namely: why was I so afraid of boredom? And more importantly, **why the heck was I going to all these events that were so boring I had to drink to get through them?!**

Sobriety brings so many gifts, and one I especially love is its ability to surprise us - to bring a new perspective and appreciation when we least expect it.

What upcoming event are you most worried about? Your birthday, a trip, a certain date on the calendar?

What if - despite your every belief in the opposite - sobriety actually made it *better*?

PLAY ALONG WITH ME...

What are your biggest fears about socialising sober?

Are you nervous about what people will say or think? Are you worried about what this decision will mean for your friendships or social life? Are you confused about what to do with your hands, or how to stay awake until the early hours? I feel you! Unleash your deepest fears onto this page and set your heart free.

ON THE FLIP SIDE

What are your biggest hopes about socialising sober?

I know you're scared. I was too. But there's a part of you that believes sobriety might actually be a *good* thing. What do you imagine might be more enjoyable? Deeper connections with people? Looking as lovely when you leave the party as you did when you walked in? Feeling proud of yourself when you get home? Explore your biggest hopes and dreams here:

_____

_____

_____

_____

_____

_____

_____

_____

_____

_____

_____

_____

_____

DECLUTTER YOUR CALENDAR

Here's another little truth bomb that might just blow your socks off:

You don't have to go to every event. The earth will still continue to turn if you miss a few.

Yes, *even if* (like me), you've always been known as the life of the party or your group's social organiser. *You don't have to be that person anymore.*

There will be many other parties and functions in your future - events you might actually enjoy more once you feel stronger in your sobriety. It's okay to sit some out.

Remember when you were a kid and you had to go to all those events you hated? For me, it was certain parties, BBQs, and sports carnivals. *Ohhh*, how this little bookworm dreaded swimming carnivals.

Well, guess what? *You're* in charge of your life now!

You can still be a nice person with good intentions and say no.

You can leave white space in your schedule, simply because it's great for your mental health. You can decide that anything that doesn't fill you with 'HELL YES!' excitement from the tips of your toes, is a loving no.

You can create a life you don't want to escape from.

So first, decide if you really want to go.

LET'S BEGIN

How many events do you currently have on your social calendar?

Are you excited about every single one? Be honest.

Listen, for more than two decades, I believed I was a complete and utter extrovert. If there was even the *hint* of an event happening, I was all up in it!

Of course, what failed to register was that it took gallons of Dutch Courage to get me there, precisely because it went against my true nature.

It was only when I stopped drinking that I realised, with blinding clarity, that the sensitive, introverted soul that had lived within me for the first 16 years of my life was still very much alive. And that perhaps cramming my calendar with social events wasn't really serving my highest good.

If you're feeling the same way, take a deep look at your upcoming events and whether you feel it's healthy for you to attend. If you feel uncomfortable about a party, BBQ or function, that feeling is enough of a sign. It's not disloyal to have these feelings. If you're new to alcohol-free life, your sobriety needs to be your main priority.

Think about how these parties or get-togethers played out in the past.

HERE'S A CLUE...

What was your initial reaction to the invitation? Before your mind had a chance to rationalise, or create a list of expectations as to what you should do. Before it started running away with FOMO (the fear of missing out).

What did your gut say?

Was your first instinct... *enthusiasm?* Or did it feel more like dread?

Listen to your intuition.

A 'should' is not a 'HELL YES!'.

Above all, avoid overwhelm right now. You have one job (to stay sober). Grant yourself that gift. Everything else can wait. You don't have to be everything to everyone.

Trim your calendar and trust your instincts.

Rule of thumb: if you have to talk yourself into it or justify it, the proposition clearly wasn't that good to begin with.

You don't *have* to go to any event that you're dreading, or don't feel ready for.

01 LET'S EXPLORE...

How many events do you currently have on your social calendar?

Which events are you most excited about, and why? What is it about these events that appeals to you most?

TREPIDATION

If you're honest, which events are less inclined to make your toes tingle?

Which invitations feel heavy, or fill you with dread?

NOT SO MUCH

What is it about these particular events that doesn't excite you?

Is it the long running time? The people invited? The logistics of getting yourself to and from the event (especially if it involves staying over at someone's house)?

_____

_____

_____

_____

_____

_____

_____

_____

_____

_____

_____

_____

_____

KEEP GOING...

Think about how many events you feel is the maximum amount that you can handle and still feel joyful, rested, and sane. Is that number: one event per week? A total of six throughout the month?

What number feels fun and uplifting for you, and why?

SWEEP THE SCENE

Knowing that some events (like a quick coffee date with a friend) may run for a lot less time than others (like a wedding), **do you feel like your upcoming social calendar is well balanced and manageable?**

If not, what do you need to change?

_____

_____

_____

_____

_____

_____

_____

_____

_____

_____

_____

_____

_____

_____

FACEBOOK FANTASYLAND

Okay, so you've picked the events you DO want to attend. Now what?

Before we go any further, let's chat about social media - or what I like to call **Facebook Fantasyland.**

Don't get me wrong. The ability to stay connected 24/7 with friends and family is magical.

But a whole new world opened up for us in the technology age, and not all of it is so crash-hot for our self-esteem.

In the space of two short decades, our brains have all but exploded with the possibilities and exhaustion of trying to keep up with everyone else's highlights reels.

The problem with social media is that it can be so easy to get sucked into 'Comparisonitis' and FOMO mode.

Photos of champagne celebrations pop up on our Facebook feed, and the beast in our head immediately starts spouting nonsense like, *"Why are you making life so hard for yourself? You're missing out! Everyone else is doing it. Just have a drink, for crying out loud!"*.

Of course, what we *don't* see are photos of the arguments, shame, and self-loathing; the horrific hangovers, embarrassing text messages, or regrets.

HERE ARE TWO EXAMPLES THAT ROCKED MY WORLD

Many moons ago, I saw a photo posted on Facebook.

My friend Sarah was more of an acquaintance, really. We ran in the same social circles and had been out drinking together more nights than I could count, but we'd never spent any real time together one-on-one.

The photo was of Sarah and her husband locked in a passionate embrace. They were on a tropical beach somewhere, and as the sun set behind them, their smiles were lit up in a golden glow of happiness.

As I looked at this beautiful photo, I felt a sudden, gnawing sense of **longing**. The setting was so idyllic and they looked so in love, I'll admit, I was envious. Suddenly my own relationship (and life) didn't quite measure up.

A few weeks later, when I heard that Sarah and her husband were getting divorced, I couldn't believe my ears. **But they looked so happy in that photo!**

The truth was, that photo was just a snapshot in time. It didn't tell the full story. It was a highlight, not the complete reality.

This lesson was shocking to me and I swore I'd always remember it.

FAST FORWARD A FEW YEARS AND INTO MY EARLY SOBRIETY

Choosing not to attend an event, I made the rookie mistake of scrolling on Facebook instead.

Instantly my feed was filled with photos of what looked like the best party in the history of the entire world.

And I had missed it! What a fool.

All night, I moped around the house, wondering what my life had come to.

It was only the next morning when a friend called, that I learnt those photos were taken well before 10pm.

Well before several friends got into a heated argument that resulted in two of them leaving in tears. And well before the soul-crushing, heart-wrenching hangovers had set in that my friend was also suffering.

Once again, that photo was just a snapshot in time. It didn't tell the full story.

IN REAL LIFE

Have you ever experienced a *social media vs. reality* lesson like this?

What happened? What did this experience teach you?

IF YOU CHOOSE NOT TO GO, UNPLUG!

If you skip an event or decide to leave early, resist the urge to drown yourself in Facebook Fantasyland.

Remember: social media pics only show the highlights - not the headaches, lost belongings or drama.

Consider temporarily deleting social media apps off your phone, or - even better - unplug yourself! Switch off your phone completely and do something that'll make you feel amazing instead.

Here are some ideas to get you started. Feel free to add your own!

Cook a special meal	*Chat with friends and family*
Read a great book	*Take a walk in nature*
Head to an exercise class	*Play with your pets*
Journal your thoughts	*Yoga, meditation or breathing exercises*
Care for your garden	

Part 2:

Prep like a Sober Rockstar

"I'd learnt an important lesson over the previous few years... It was that having a great toolbox of support could mean the difference between weeping alone in the corner, and rocking it out and actually enjoying the challenge. Before embarking on a lifestyle change of this magnitude, I knew I'd need help, and lots of it.
Before next weekend arrived, I was going to need a Serious Action Plan."

– *A Happier Hour*

BOOST YOUR HAPPY VIBES

Okay, so now you know which events you want to go to. Great! Ready to prep for your upcoming event like a sober superstar? Slip into scrumptious self-care!

In the days leading up to the event, boost your bliss vibes and get your confidence and energy flowing.

Do things that make you feel good: exercise more, meditate, make love, listen to uplifting tunes, get a little sunshine and lots of sleep, play games with your pet, or chat with your favourite people.

When you feel well-cared for, energised, and happy, you're much more likely to feel like socialising.

Moving your body is an especially great trick for getting all your nervous jiggles out pre-event, and helping you to feel relaxed.

Running is super popular with the newly sober because it can deliver those feelings of 'carefree' freedom we were forever seeking at the bottom of the bottle (without all the downsides).

Moving your body:

- gets the blood and endorphins pumping
- is a natural stress reliever
- helps you feel and sleep better
- makes your skin glow and your eyes sparkle
- provides a holistic high and a rush of confidence and energy, so you're ready for socialising!

02 MAGICAL MOVEMENT

The great news is you don't have to drag your butt to the gym if you hate it. Find movement you love! There are so many incredible classes and activities you can try. Round up a friend and make it an adventure. Experiment until you find a type of movement that feels fun and pleasurable to you.

What kind of exercise do you love most?

EXPERIMENTAL EXERCISE

What type of exercise would you like to try next?

Think outside the box. Maybe you'd like to experience aerial yoga, canoeing, rock climbing, trampolining, or dance classes. The world's your oyster!

_____

_____

_____

_____

_____

_____

_____

_____

_____

_____

_____

_____

_____

_____

NOURISHING YOUR BODY

Above all else, *avoiding alcohol is your number one priority right now.*

But as much as possible, in the days leading up to the event (and in general, really), reduce processed and fast food, refined sugar, gluten, dairy, caffeine and simple carbs (like white bread, cakes, and pastries). They'll only zap your energy and make you feel worse.

Instead, fill up on:

Small, Regular Meals. Well-balanced and brimming with simple, whole foods, fresh from nature.

Healthy Snacks. Try fresh fruit kebabs, veggie sticks with hummus, or a DIY trail mix with toasted nuts and seeds.

Sweet, root vegetables (like carrot, beets, pumpkin and sweet potato) have a soothing, grounding effect and can help to alleviate sugar cravings.

Protein works to balance blood glucose and energy levels (pure magic before you head to an event). Great sources include eggs, meat, tofu, chickpeas, and quinoa.

Good Fats nourish your brain and central nervous system (goodbye anxiety and jitters!). Indulge in plenty of avocados, olives, extra-virgin olive oil, coconut, coconut oil, nuts and seeds (and their butters, like almond butter or tahini).

PRE-EVENT NUTRITION PLAN

The meal you eat before you head to an event can be especially crucial.

Giving yourself the gift of highly nutritious foods can mean the difference between dragging yourself through a party, and actually shaking your booty on the dance floor!

What are your favourite healthy foods? **What will you eat before you head to your next event?** Jot down some meal ideas here...

Menu

02 GET FRIENDLY WITH H₂O

Hydrate that beautiful bod of yours! Water works to boost your mood and energy levels, and flushes out the toxins so you can feel better faster.

Don't worry if plain water's not your thing. You can make it more delicious by infusing it.

Simply combine a large jug or bottle of still or sparkling water with a handful of fresh or frozen fruits or herbs. Leave for a few hours (or overnight) to infuse. Then, strain and enjoy!

Mix and match slices and sprigs of your favourites:

Lime	Blueberries
Cucumber	Strawberries
Mint leaves	Lemon
Orange	Mango
Basil Leaves	Peach

SOBER TREATS

If you're anything like me, up until this point, alcohol was always your reward. *Had a hard day? You deserve a drink. Time to celebrate? Bring on the drink!*

It can be tough to retrain your brain. **That's where sober treats can help!**

What the heck are sober treats, you ask? Anything you want them to be!

Think of them as little gifts of appreciation for doing this brave thing. Pepper your steps along the way with small treats like fresh flowers, great quality chocolate, a bubble bath, a tin of herbal tea, pretty nail polish, a ripe peach or fresh pineapple, a new book or magazine, music, a new journal, scented candle, or essential oil room spray.

These treats are your reward for remaining sober.

These treats are vital because without them, sobriety doesn't feel like fun or an adventure - it feels like deprivation.

Not only is this practice about treating yourself like the rockstar you are, but it also sets a new standard of self-care that will enrich every area of your life.

It helps you to avoid feeling depleted or resentful, and reinforces positive behaviour. It serves as a reminder of this new life you are creating, and even has the power to provide you with a new wonder for all the small, ordinary, magical things in life.

TINY TREATS AND SOBER REWARDS IDEAS

Does a particular treat come to mind for you? What are a couple of treats you might start with?

Be generous with yourself. It can be so easy to disregard how much we once spent on drinks and cabs and late-night feasts. We might find it hard to justify buying a new book or fancy sparkling water drinks, forgetting that we never thought twice about buying a crate of champagne, or shouting drinks for everyone at the bar.

_____

_____

_____

_____

_____

_____

_____

_____

_____

_____

_____

FAREWELL, FOMO!

Okay, before we go any further, let's address the big elephant in the room. *How do you avoid feeling resentment or having FOMO over the fact that everyone else will be drinking?!*

The thing about this fear of missing out is that it lies in **the belief that sobriety equals a life of deprivation or punishment.**

That is, you fear that everyone else will be imbibing and you'll be missing out on some special thing. You feel envious that they can do as they like, while you're forcing yourself to "be good".

But here's the thing: **this fear is misplaced.**

You're not really scared you'll miss out - you can still go to everything you're invited to. You can still laugh with your friends and dance yourself silly. What you're *really* scared of is that everyone else will have more fun than you, because you still believe drinking is more fun than sobriety.

Which means it's not your friends or your invitations that need to change (necessarily); it's your *mindset*.

And a brilliant way to reframe this? **Make your option more fun!**

When you love your own choice, you no longer feel like you're missing out on anything.

So how do we do that? How do we make it more fun?

Let's get started!

GO-TO GOODIES!

A savvy trick of the sober socialite? Have goodies waiting for you when you get home!

Yep, all those delicious little treats and rewards we just talked about.

Maybe you love scented candles and a great book, or fresh sheets on the bed.

I love knowing I can have raw desserts waiting for me in the freezer, so even if the event's a fizzer, I still have something to look forward to!

When you get home and enjoy your treat, remind yourself that this is your reward for remaining sober.

Socialising sober can be tough at first! Really romance yourself through it.

Another strategy is to invest the money saved by not drinking, into little upgrades. Especially if it's a big event you're dreading but can't get out of, like a compulsory work function, or a distant relative's wedding.

Ask yourself: *how can you make the event more fun?*

You might like to upgrade an experience (by investing in better seats or tickets), upgrade food (choosing a nicer restaurant), or accommodation (springing for an extra star). Trust me, you'll notice and appreciate all the little upgrades so much more, now that you're completely conscious.

STANDARDS SHIFT

None of this stuff might have mattered to us back when we were drinking, of course. I would've quite happily slept on a mattress on a relative's floor if it meant I could drink myself silly all night.

But when we embrace sobriety, *well*... **our standards shift.** We start to notice little things, like how loud the neighbours are, or how tiring it is to socialise for twelve hours straight. We start to crave the squishy comforts that make us feel safe and well-cared for.

When Dom and I were recently invited to a wedding scheduled to run for over nine hours, I'll be honest, my first reaction was dread. So rather than just driving the 45 minutes or so to the event, I booked a nearby hotel - for both the night *before*, and the night *of* the wedding.

I figured if there was a pool and a day spa, I'd have plenty of fun options to book-end the wedding with, to ensure the whole event felt like a fun treat.

If you know an event is going to be particularly challenging, investing in some extra little touches will remind you how much you value yourself now, and how worthy you are of beautiful hotel rooms, a bed of your own, or seats with more leg room on the plane.

02 HOME SWEET HOME

What have you prepared to ensure your home (or even just your bedroom!) is a delight to return to? What goodies will you have waiting for you when you get home?

- [ ] Scented candles.
- [ ] Clean sheets.
- [ ] A great book.

- [ ] Fresh flowers.
- [ ] Fancy chocolates.
- [ ] Herbal tea.

MAKE IT MORE FUN!

If your event involves travel, let's go one step further! Will you:

☐ *Upgrade the experience (a VIP pass or better tickets).*

☐ *Upgrade the food (choosing a nicer restaurant).*

☐ *Upgrade your accommodation.*

☐ *Upgrade your seat on the plane/train/coach.*

☐ _____

☐ _____

☐ _____

☐ _____

☐ _____

☐ _____

☐ _____

☐ _____

MAGICAL MORNINGS

Another way to boost your enthusiasm as you head into each event? **Make a sublime plan for the following morning!**

Book a ticket or make a plan for something you'll really look forward to – an activity that'll feel delicious to wake up to when you're feeling fresh and hangover-free.

Maybe that's a long walk with your loved one(s), or breakfast in an ocean side cafe. Maybe it's just a little time out for yourself – time to curl up with a fancy coffee and a book in the sunshine.

For me, sometimes it's a fun yoga or hula hooping class in the park. Sometimes it's a smoothie date with a friend, or some kind of art, crafting, or decluttering project (heaven for my inner geek!).

During each event, if you feel tempted to drink (especially if you find yourself being triggered by the people drinking around you), picture your morning-after plan and how much you'll enjoy it with a clear head.

It's like having a delicious little secret, *just for you.*

YOUR SUBLIME MORNING-AFTER

What plans would you like to make for the morning after the event?

Brainstorm some ideas here, then pick up the phone and make it happen!

Part 3:

Mindset Shifts

"I thought about the question Dom asked me when I first told him about the beast. *What are you really craving?*

Deep down, I knew it wasn't actually the alcohol itself. So what was it? That feeling of letting loose; of wild abandon? Or the sense of connection I thought I got when I drank with people?

==Was I really craving more fun, adventure, affection, and freedom in my life?"==

– *A Happier Hour*

MAGICAL REFRAMING

Okedokey, now that your body and environment are ready, let's talk grey matter.

In early sobriety, **having the right perspective is everything.**

Let's face it, embarking on any big life change is bound to be challenging. Not only are we creating new neural pathways in our brain, but we're also learning how to interact with the world in a whole new way. That's some powerful stuff!

It's normal to feel terrified of all this change, and in the process, to find ourselves imagining the worst.

Our minds can be incredibly powerful in helping us to overcome fears and old patterns, and training our brains to focus on the positive can really supercharge our efforts.

In other words, having powerful ways to reframe our thinking can mean the difference between actually *enjoying* our sobriety endeavour, and sinking back into old habits that no longer serve us.

So how do we flip the switch?

Here are two of my favourite strategies:

1. Ask the right question.
2. Stay focused on your 'why'.

Let's dive in...

1. ASK THE RIGHT QUESTION

Back when I was desperately trying (and failing) to moderate my drinking, I'd go around and around in my (hungover) head, thinking:

Well, it's not like I'm a falling-down-in-the-gutter drunk, or anything. I haven't lost my job, or crashed my car... Surely I don't have to give it up **completely?!**

Turns out I was asking entirely the wrong question. The right one – the one that shifted everything – was:

What was I giving up by continuing to drink?

This was such a powerful reframe. It didn't require a label, or an ultimatum, or just one more quiz about whether or not I drank too much.

Deep down, I knew the truth. Drinking took more away from my life than it was giving. It didn't make me happy or fill me with joy. It negatively impacted my relationships, self-worth, career, creativity, and health. Alcohol wasn't good for me and I was much better off without it.

Continually asking, *"Am I really that bad?"* wasn't the key to a new perspective or the happiness I craved.

Instead, asking, *"Is this situation **good** enough for me, and the life I truly want?"* allowed me to see things through fresh eyes, and move forward in a whole new way.

As you practice socialising sober (and find yourself bravely doing things you never believed you could!), continue to ask the right question. It has the power to deliver miracles.

2. STAY FOCUSED ON YOUR 'WHY'

Why do you want to live alcohol-free?

Having firm reasons in your mind as to *why* you're on this sober safari in the first place, can help immensely when it comes to keeping you inspired and on track.

Your reasons can act as a compass, helping you to focus on the bigger picture and your overall intentions. They can offer protection against triggers and temptations, or those pesky little thoughts like: *'Oh what does it matter? One won't hurt.'*

My reasons included wanting to pour my heart and soul into something (the small business I was creating) for the first time in my life, and be able to say I gave it my all. I also wanted to experience a richer, deeper relationship with my love, and just between you and me, I was more than a little concerned about my impending 40th birthday.

I didn't want to be a loudmouth lush anymore! I didn't want my drinking to keep holding me back. I didn't want to feel upset if I couldn't have a drink on Friday nights. I didn't want to keep falling into the binge drinking trap. I was sick of the anxiety, the shame, and the horrific hangovers slowing me down and keeping me from rocking my passions.

I wanted *freedom!* I wanted to feel playful, with confidence that was *real* and *palpable*. I wanted deeper relationships, less anxiety, more space, more love, more potential. I craved *transformation!*

How about you?

BUT, WHY?

Maybe your reasons include being a better role model to your kids; improving your health and actually *enjoying* your weekends rather than spending them hungover; to follow your dreams, reach your potential and find out what you're truly made of; or to be a kinder and more patient friend, wife, sister, colleague, or mother. **Let your reasons guide you.**

WHY do you want to live alcohol-free? What are your biggest inspirations, motivators or driving forces for this new chapter?

_____

_____

_____

_____

_____

_____

_____

_____

_____

_____

_____

_____

_____

GREAT! NOW DIG DEEPER...

If someone questions you (*aka: peer pressure!*), it pays to know what your reasons are, and believe in them.

What do you stand to gain by remaining sober? Before your head has a chance to run away with fear, review the evidence: what benefits have you experienced in sobriety so far? What else do you believe will improve, with enough time sober?

Really sink into this question. Think about all aspects of your life: health, creativity, career, relationships, finances, spirituality, etc.

03 BEYOND DOUBT

Conversely, what will you be giving up if you continue to drink?

What are all the down-sides or consequences of drinking in your life? What will your life look like if you don't choose sobriety? What will you be missing out on by continuing to drink?

_____

_____

_____

_____

_____

_____

_____

_____

_____

_____

_____

_____

_____

_____

SETTING YOUR INTENTIONS

Back when I worked in the corporate world, we were encouraged to take a 'Defensive Driving' course that involved performing a variety of manoeuvres on a racetrack.

In one of the exercises, we were instructed to speed up, and then slam on the brakes and avoid hitting a particular safety cone.

Despite our best efforts, we all hit that cone.

Next, we tried the activity again, but this time, rather than focusing on the cone, we were instructed to look for a safe place to steer the car. Same distance, same speed, same brakes; just a different intention and focus.

We were *stunned*. Every single one of us avoided the cone.

Our instructor explained that if something or someone jumps out in front of us, the worst thing we can do is look straight at it as we're trying to avoid it.

We need to focus on where we *want* to go, rather than where we *don't* want to go.

The lesson was powerful and I often find myself telling this story. Time and again, I notice that when we focus on our fears, we tend to smash into them.

And if we're not focusing on where we really want to go, how can we expect to get there?

03 VISUALISATION IS KEY

There's a great reason that top athletes and entrepreneurs use this tool for success - *because it works!*

When it comes to drinking, how many times did you give yourself a lecture about not making a fool of yourself this time, or not letting the night get too messy... only to find that's exactly where you ended up?

Too many to count? Me too.

The beautiful thing about visualisation is that we can use it anywhere, anytime, to help keep our sense of humour (and sanity!) firmly intact.

Including right now!

> **Try this:**
>
> Close your eyes for a moment and take a deep breath. Become aware of how your body feels. Now imagine yourself one month / three months / one year from now: joyful, healthy and empowered. Picture yourself radiant and ready to take on anything.

HOW DOES IT *FEEL?*

What words and emotions come up for you? Do you visualise yourself feeling confident, loving, clear-minded, light, carefree, strong, energised, glowing, calm, cheerful, excited, feminine, or brave?

Or perhaps you see yourself feeling balanced, glamorous, sensual, liberated, joyful, nourished, relaxed, whole, spirited, or empowered?

If we're completely honest, it was rarely the alcohol *itself* that we craved in any situation. It was that we wanted to *feel* (or *not* feel) a certain way.

When we don't feel the way we want to, it's only natural to crave an easy escape. As humans, we're hard-wired to gravitate towards pleasure, and avoid painful, unpleasant emotions at all costs!

What if 'controlling your drinking' doesn't mean learning how to moderate, but creating a life so complete and fulfilling that alcohol can't add anything you don't already have?

What if that's what this sobriety expedition is really all about? Creating a life - and a relationship with yourself - that you don't want to run away from?

This one little question - **how do you want to *feel?*** - has the power to guide you there.

03
MOOD BOARD

What are two words of intention that inspire you most?

For example, the two emotions and feelings that inspired me most in early sobriety were: *playful* and *radiant*. I longed to live an alcohol-free life full of fun and vibrance. I wanted to feel deeply happy and healthy. **How do you want to feel?**

EXPLORE THE MEANING

To me, playful meant creativity, fun, spontaneity, mischief, and joy. Radiant meant sparkly, healthy, glowing, connected, and blissful.

Brainstorm here. **What do your words, emotions, and intentions mean to you?**

_____

_____

_____

_____

_____

_____

_____

_____

_____

_____

_____

_____

_____

_____

_____

HOLD THAT IMAGE IN YOUR MIND

Really soak up every little inch of it. Let the vision of how you want to feel be your blueprint; your map for where you want to steer yourself and your life. Let it guide you through every new event.

Another tip is to visualise each event. Close your eyes, take another deep breath, and visualise yourself moving gracefully through the party. See yourself laughing, socialising, and having an amazing time, alcohol-free. Soak in how fun it feels to be playful, light and free.

Imagine your clear and grateful head hitting the pillow that night. Envisage how heavenly you'll feel the next morning (especially as you enjoy your morning-after treat!). And revel in how flippin' *proud* of yourself you feel.

Fun, right?

The best part about visualising is that you can practice this anywhere: at work, on the bus or train, in bed, or anytime leading up to the event.

Put your mind to work and let the real change begin!

VISUALISE THE EVENT

How do you want to feel at your upcoming occasion, and the morning after?

When it comes to this event in particular, what mood or words of intention inspire you most? Visualise yourself there. How do other people see you? How do you see yourself?

_____

_____

_____

_____

_____

_____

_____

_____

_____

_____

_____

_____

_____

_____

08 VISUALISE THE FUTURE

How do you want to feel at an event three months from now?

Just think of all the ways you can practice between now and then. How will you be changed by all this training? How will you *feel* at events in the future? Really go to town with your descriptions - this stuff is powerful! Focus on where you're *going*, not where you've been.

FAST-FORWARD GAME

We're not done with our brains just yet! This simple mindset exercise can really help to shine a bold light on the truth about drinking.

Aaahhh, alcohol. So glamorous, so romantic, so seductive... or *is it?*

Another way to ensure you have a rock solid mindset going into any event is to play the 'Fast Forward' game.

Here's how. Think past the first 'romantic' image of drinking, and focus on the reality of what the event actually ends up being like. That is, start by imagining the supposed 'glamour' and 'romance' of drinking - and finish with your worst case scenario (arguments with loved ones, embarrassment, or regret).

Because, deep down we all know how it's likely to end, right?

Okay, I'll go first, shall I?

Then feel free to share your own stories and examples. Brutal, liberating honesty. Write it all out, and set yourself free...

REAL WORLD EXAMPLES

Opening Scene:

One of my closest friends is in town for the day and I'm so excited to meet her. I'm all dolled up in my favourite frock and we meet at a fancy waterfront venue in the city. We hug and squeal, and giggle over our first bottle of bubbles, feeling foot-loose and fancy-free.

Fast-Forward:

It's only 5pm, we've already polished off three bottles, and are completely smashed. People stream into the venue, fresh from work. Meanwhile, we are a sloppy, emotional mess.

My friend has told me a ton of personal news throughout the day, none of which I'll remember. We decide to go home, and attempt a farewell hug on the street before I fall into a cab.

When I arrive home, I stagger straight past Dom and pass out, face-down on the couch. I wake up at 3am, and spend the next few hours staring at the ceiling with my dehydrated head pounding, wondering why the hell I keep doing this to myself.

READY FOR ANOTHER EXAMPLE?

Opening Scene:

Dom and I are off to a friend's party! We haven't caught up with everyone in so long and I'm so looking forward to seeing them and hearing everyone's news.

Dom has already given me the *'now, just take it easy'* talk on the cab ride over, but it's *fine*, I already gave myself that lecture as I got ready. I feel confident and happy as I accept my first drink.

Fast-Forward:

It's 10pm and I'm drunk and disorientated. I feel like no-one wants to talk to me, and I don't know why. I try to strike up a new conversation but I'm too loud, or they're too loud, or *something*.

I figure I should just dance instead, and shake myself around on the dance floor until I get too dizzy. I sit down on the cozy couch for a while to 'rest my eyes'.

I vaguely remember Dom dragging me into a taxi. I wake up the next morning filled with shame and dread, wondering if I owe anyone an apology and cringing at the thought of how I must have looked. I scramble around on the floor trying to locate my phone and search for clues, only to discover I've lost my handbag…

08 YOUR TURN

Ugh. This exercise can cause quite the thud down to earth, huh? But it's also an incredibly powerful reminder of all the mayhem drinking can cause. All the pain, all the lost time... *Glamorous?* Hardly!

Ok, your turn. Explore the exercise here, and really let it rip with the second part. **How did those 'fun' drinking events often go for you,** *really?*

Opening Scene:

AND THEN WHAT HAPPENED?

Fast-Forward:

LET'S EXPLORE ANOTHER EXAMPLE

Opening Scene:

AND THEN...

Fast-Forward:

Great work! Now take a photo of this journal on your phone and pull it out whenever you walk past a bar, see people sipping drinks in the sunshine, or begin to feel that old, familiar longing.

Let this journal remind you of the messy truth about drinking, beyond the imagined glamour and romance of it all.

08
FLIP IT FORWARD

You know what's even better than reminding yourself how awful alcohol can be? Reminding yourself just how wonderful sobriety can be!

Flip the Fast Forward Game on its head this time and picture what it'll feel like to wake up the next morning, still sober and smug as a bug! How does the night begin? **How do you set yourself up for sober success?**

Opening Scene:

NOW FOR THE FUN PART

Fast-Forward:

Imagine how it feels to come home (and more importantly, wake up!) completely sober. How will you feel the next day; relieved, proud, hopeful? What will this win mean for your sobriety intentions and, more importantly, how you feel about yourself?

_____

_____

_____

_____

_____

_____

_____

_____

_____

_____

Way to go! Play fast forward on that scene!

This is the real glamour and excitement, right here. Sober living in bold, vibrant technicolour.

Part 4:

Get This Party Started!

"Shifting my focus to what I was gaining, rather than what I was giving up, helped me to feel empowered."

– *A Happier Hour*

PERFECT PLAYLIST

This is it! The day of the event has arrived and you feel your nerves skyrocketing.

Don't panic! A few more steps of prep will have you dancing your way into the party with sky-high confidence and good cheer.

And on that fun note, it's time to crank your favourite playlist!

As curious as it sounds, ending our relationship with alcohol can feel eerily similar to the heartbreak of ending any other relationship.

I truly grieved the loss in my life at first. I cried because I missed drinking. I cried because I couldn't imagine the rest of my life without it.

I felt devastated that something so stupid could have such an incredible hold over me. And sometimes seeing other people drinking felt exactly like seeing an ex-boyfriend, and all the emotions came flooding back.

But just like with any breakup, it gets easier. You cry, you avoid them, and then you start rebuilding your life.

And a musical trick that can help the process along?

Breakup songs!

TURN IT UP

As two of our Sexy Sobriety Members shared:

" Associating drinking with a bad relationship helps me greatly. I'm a huge music fan and love 'angry chick songs' about bad relationships.
My favorite thing to do when I'm singing along at the top of my lungs in the car is to replace the 'boyfriend' with the bottle or alcohol! I tell ya, it works for every breakup song and helps to get that angst out and remind myself that I am a badass!
The absolute best song to switch out the person with alcohol is Fighter by Christina Aguilera! So empowering. Listen to every word, it totally works! "

" I actually built a whole Spotify playlist for this purpose! I call it "Roar," and over time it has grown to over 150 songs.
I started by only adding songs with upbuilding lyrics. The way I see it, singing is like repeating affirmations over and over, so might as well make them a positive message! "

I love this concept so much, and they're right - it absolutely works! I love to picture the face of The Beast (or the Wine Witch!) whenever I sing:

- Hit Me With Your Best Shot - Pat Benatar *(okay, so that one probably ages me, ha!)*.
- I'm Still Standing - Elton John
- Since You've Been Gone - Kelly Clarkson
- Stronger - Kelly Clarkson *(I mean, pretty much any of Kelly's songs, right?)*

SOBER WARRIOR SONGS

Give it a try! Jot your favourites down here, including how empowered they make you feel. Which songs are your all-time favourites?

Songs for pumping up my confidence in the days leading up to an event (maybe even while working out all my nervous wiggles at the gym!):

Songs for boosting my resolve on the day of an event, and dancing around to while getting ready:

04 SING IT, SISTER!

Songs for settling my nerves or building my excitement to as I drive to an event:

Songs for chilling out and celebrating the morning after an event:

THE POWER OF GRATITUDE

Journaling is a tool that can help us to process complicated emotions and deal with them in a healthier way, and a gratitude journal, in particular, can help shift our perspective in a jiffy.

Writing a short list of things you're grateful for is practically *guaranteed* to make you feel better.

Maybe you like to record the happiest moment of each day, helping you to see the silver linings in even the biggest challenges. Or maybe you prefer to write about what you're learning about yourself – and *life* – each day.

One journal prompt I totally love is: **"Because I was sober today, I …"**

Not only is this a beautiful twist on the regular gratitude practice, but it also helps to reinforce new (healthier!) patterns of behaviour.

Better yet, it gives you recorded evidence of just how brave you're being every single day - and that sobriety is enriching your life in more ways than you ever thought possible.

For example, because I was sober today, I watched a beautiful sunrise, went for a long walk with my love, had the energy and wherewithal to help other people, read a few chapters of a (surprisingly funny) new book, and shared a long laugh with a good friend. Most of all, I felt completely relaxed and at home in my own skin.

How about you?

04 BLISSFUL GRATITUDE

Reflecting on all the good things in your life that you feel thankful for is a great way to boost your confidence. **The better you feel about yourself and your life, the more fun you'll have while socialising sober.**

Try writing in this gratitude journal every day for a week, and watch what happens!

MONDAY

I'm grateful to my body for...

_____

_____

TUESDAY

A person in my life I'm grateful for is...

_____

_____

WEDNESDAY

The happiest moment of my day was...

_____

_____

APPRECIATION LOVE NOTES

THURSDAY

A lesson I'm grateful for is...

FRIDAY

I'm so grateful that...

SATURDAY

A memory I'm grateful to have is...

SUNDAY

Because I was sober today, I...

SELF CARE TRAVEL KIT

Next up? Get packing!

It's entirely possible your socialising plans involve visiting other people's houses, or heading to venues where you can take a few things with you.

If so, great!

Packing a Self-Care Travel Kit can provide that little bit of extra comfort and reassurance. It can serve as a great reminder that you have your own back - that you can trust yourself now to take care of yourself.

You can pack anything you like into your Self-Care Travel Kit - anything that makes you feel safe and cared for. But there are 3 things in particular I always love to take with me...

1. A fully charged phone (with all accessories).
2. Power-packed lists.
3. Snacks and elixirs.

Grab your favourite bag, and let's start packing...

1. A FULLY CHARGED PHONE

Pre-loaded with positive and inspiring inputs, pack your phone, headphones - and your charger if your event involves travel or spans many hours.

Doing just about *anything* for the first time is scary, right? But once you make the leap, a whole new world opens up for you.

So let your phone be your source of inspiration and hope while you get the hang of this sober-socialising thing.

Before you leave home, download or save any relevant bookmarks. Make sure all your subscriptions are up to date, and you can log into any websites or online programs you might need to support you.

Then, any time it all gets too much or you just need a little breather, you can go for a walk (or hide yourself in the garden or bathroom) for ten minutes and:

- Call a friend
- Sink into a guided meditation
- Watch an inspiring video
- Listen to a podcast, audiobook, or relaxing music
- Read an uplifting ebook

You might also like to line up a few episodes of your favourite comedy shows or podcasts to watch or listen to as you get ready for the event.

Dom and I often listen to funny audiobooks as we drive to events - it helps to get us in the mood and boost our sense of humour!

04 PRELOADED

Fill in this checklist before you head to each event, and you'll know you're ready to weather any storm!

Is your phone ready to go the distance with you?

- [ ] Is it fully charged, complete with headphones?

- [ ] If the event involves travel or spans many hours, do you have your charger or battery pack with you?

- [ ] Do you have enough data left, or do you need to top up?

- [ ] Have you downloaded or saved all relevant episodes, links, or bookmarks?

- [ ] Do you have a range of options to choose from depending on your mood, including funny videos, inspiring podcasts, audiobooks, ebooks, etc.?

- [ ] Do you have your best friend, family member, or support person on speed dial, just in case?

- [ ] Are all your subscriptions are up to date, and can you log into any websites or online programs you might want to use to help support you through the event?

2. POWER-PACKED LISTS

If you're a list person like me, taking your lists with you can really keep you on track and help you to sidestep triggers.

When I first socialised sober, I took one list with me in particular: **Ten Things Better than Booze.**

My list included things like:

- Productive, happy mornings. No headaches, no hangovers – just bliss.
- Powerful clarity – of thoughts, emotions, energy.
- Better digestion. Absorption of every last trace of that expensive Spirulina!
- Stronger memories and regret-free FUN!
- Deep conversations, and deliciously spontaneous giggles.
- Personal growth. Because nothing changes until we do.

Then, whenever I was feeling shaky during an event, I'd pull out my list and remind myself of all the reasons I wanted to embrace sobriety - all the things I was working towards, and looking forward to. *The woman I wanted to be.*

The thing is, when we're surrounded by people drinking, we can tend to develop temporary amnesia and all our best intentions can go flying right out the window.

So don't let them!

Write out your own list of motivators, and then take it (or a photo using your phone) with you.

10 THINGS BETTER THAN BOOZE

Think: heavenly mornings, glowing skin and eyes that sparkle, deeper relationships, the smell of fresh, clean sheets beneath your clear and happy head as you fall sleep...

What would you add?

1. _____
2. _____
3. _____
4. _____
5. _____
6. _____
7. _____
8. _____
9. _____
10. _____

3. SNACKS AND ELIXIRS

Snacks are especially important if you're travelling long distances to get to the event or staying over at someone else's house.

There's an acronym often used in recovery circles: HALT - reminding us that getting hungry, angry, lonely, or tired can all act as triggers, and that we might want to put an action plan in place to protect ourselves from those states.

As funny as it sounds, when we're hungry, we can become emotional, and when we're emotional, we can feel triggered to drink.

I always love to pack a few muesli bars, protein balls, bananas, crackers, or nuts to take with me.

When we're newly sober, we need a little extra TLC to avoid falling back into old patterns, so consider packing snacks for yourself like you would if you were caring for a toddler (and wanted to avoid regular meltdowns!).

Healthier options will keep your energy up, but even some salty, crunchy snacks might help if you suspect you might be super stressed or anxious.

DRINK DELIGHTS

Before you go to each event, check with the venue to see if they offer a range of non-alcoholic drinks. If they don't, you could ask if you can bring your own.

You might feel strange doing it, but most places don't mind (especially if they already have a corkage fee anyway), and taking your own means you can join in with your friends and not be stuck drinking plain water or sugary sodas all night.

If it's a BBQ, house party, or some other kind of bring-your-own event you're headed to, even better! Now you're free to take plenty of alcohol-free options with you. Check out your local grocery store before you go - there are so many ready-made drinks on the market today and many of them are really good!

Also consider taking mockail ingredients, like freshly squeezed juice, sparkling mineral or tonic water, and garnishes like fresh mint or basil, or citrus slices.

The more options you have, the less appealing booze will be.

As a bonus tip: take extra supplies so you have enough to share. Every single time I've pulled out mocktails at a party, a ton of people have clambered to try them. So bring more than you need, and you'll be one very happy (and popular) party guest!

Plus, of course, if *you're* the one hosting, do all this in reverse: make sure you have all these goodies (in surplus) within easy reach at home!

FULLY EQUIPPED

What kinds of snacks would you like to take with you?
For example: muesli bars, protein balls, bananas or dried fruit, crackers, nuts, etc?

What elixirs or mocktail ingredients will you take with you?
Consider: pre-packed alcohol-free drinks in cans or bottles? Or fruit/vegetable juice, sparking mineral or tonic water, fresh herbs like mint or basil, citrus peel or slices, etc?

Brilliant work! Now that the nitty gritty is taken care of, it's time to amp up your poise and self-assurance *(oh my!)*. **Right this way...**

Part 5:

Confidence Hacks

"I thought I needed to drink to feel confident. And yet, the longer I went without drinking, the more confident I felt in every situation. Life was so incredibly *peaceful* without all that internal angst and drama."

– *A Happier Hour*

ACTION CREATES CONFIDENCE

Once upon a time I firmly believed that alcohol equalled confidence... *right?*

That's the reason I was first in line at the bar *every single time*.

"Alcohol stands for fun! And mischief! And shenanigans!"

Until it doesn't.

Until you wake up the next morning like a bear with a sore head – your stomach sick with dread about what you might have said or done the night before.

"Did I upset anyone? Did I make an ass of myself? Oh God, where's my purse/phone/car?"

'Dutch Courage' is a diddle. *There*, I said it.

If there's one topic that comes up (time and again!) in my work helping brave souls to live alcohol-free, it's that true confidence comes from within. And that the longer we go without drinking, the more confident we feel in every situation.

Alcohol doesn't create confidence; *action* **does.**

Taking those first, scary steps. Doing things for the first time. Blowing our minds with our ever-expanding savvy and strength. *No pre-gaming necessary.*

And a fun way to get started with all that action-building confidence? **Introducing the ultimate socialising sober lifehacks...**

05 CHOOSE 3 FAVOURITES

Bring-your-own events like BBQs and house parties are fabulous, in that you can take your own drinks and ensure you have plenty of scrumptious options.

But what about all those other events, like socialising at pubs or bars, weddings, or work functions?

For these types of events, it's crucial to have a game plan for ordering drinks: to choose 3 favourites - and rehearse your bold little heart out!

Have not one, but *three* of your favourite alcohol-free drinks firmly in your mind, so you can swiftly and confidently ask for the next one if your first favourite isn't available.

Maybe you love sparkling soda water with fresh lemon, ginger ale, or cranberry juice with fresh lime.

With any luck, delicious mocktails will be on order, but if not, at least you'll have some great options ready to roll off your tongue when the waiter asks: "What'll it be?"

Have fun with it!

There's a Seinfeld episode that always makes me laugh, where Jerry places his drink order with a sassy smile, practically singing, "I'll have a cranberry juice with two limes!" Even the mental image of this drink is so much fun.

Being super specific with your order generally comes across as very confident, assuring others that you know exactly what you want. Rehearse asking for your drinks with a cheeky grin or a casual air.

ORDERING DRINKS

Remember: practice makes perfect. Socialising sober - and ordering new drinks - is a skill we can learn to master. Try out some scripts below and have fun practicing!

"What'll it be?"
What's your first drink of choice?

_____

_____

_____

"Sorry, ma'am/sir. We don't have {your first choice}. Would you like something else?"
What's your second drink of choice?

_____

_____

_____

"I'm afraid we don't have that either. Could I get you something else?"
What's your third drink of choice?

_____

_____

_____

SPOT YOUR EXITS

Okay, so fingers crossed you get to the event and have an absolute blast and don't want to leave. Wonderful!

But what if you don't?

Having an escape plan already in place can really help to put your mind at ease.

As a former party girl, I found this whole idea to be such a huge reframe. I'd always been the first to arrive at any party and the last to leave, so to realise I could actually leave earlier if I wanted to, astounded me.

And that's not all!

Another great aspect that continues to blow my mind (even now), is that you can drive! Farewell, worries about how you'll get home, or waiting for cabs in the freezing cold - you can completely take your power back!

Drive to the event if you can.

If you offer friends a lift, let them know prior that they'll need to find an alternative way home, as you might want to leave early. You might discover - like I did - that long, boozy events are too tiring for you now, and you prefer to stay for just two or three hours.

Setting expectations ahead of time means you're free as a bird to fly out of there any time you like.

KNOW YOUR OBJECTIVES

Think you might feel guilty about leaving when you want to?

Setting a bare minimum requirement for each event can help with this.

Namely, deciding ahead of time the main reasons you want to go to the event. Perhaps there's one or two things in particular that you want to do there; personal goals you'll be happy to have achieved if you decide to leave early.

This might be catching up with one friend or colleague in particular, for example. It might be simply to wish the birthday girl a great day.

When you arrive at the event, challenge yourself to complete your bare minimum requirement within the first hour.

Why, you ask? Because once you've ticked this item off, all pressure is removed and you can either choose to stay (if you're having fun), or to go home (if you're not).

Either way, you'll feel proud of yourself and glad you came, knowing you walked away having accomplished the most important thing to you at this event.

Above all else, protect your sobriety at this early stage. If that means hightailing it *outta'* there after a couple of hours, so be it! By then, everyone else is probably a few drinks in and won't mind (or notice!) anyway.

Know your limits, and listen to your body. You don't have to stay for any longer than you can cope with.

ESCAPE PLAN

Hopefully you won't need to use this plan because you'll be having too much fun, but the truth is, sometimes an event just isn't what we hoped it would be. And that's okay! Having an escape plan means you can make a graceful exit at a time that feels right to you.

How are you getting to and from the event?

Will you drive? Have you offered friends a lift, and if so, have you set the expectation ahead of time that they'll need to find their own way home?

_____

_____

_____

_____

_____

_____

_____

_____

_____

_____

_____

GOAL GETTER

What's your bare minimum requirement or goal for your event?

What's the main reason you want to go? Is there a particular friend you want to catch up with, or a couple you want to congratulate? Who do you need to seek out in the first hour of the event, so you can leave knowing you nailed it?

FROCKIN' FABULOUS!

When you feel beautiful (whatever that means to you), don't you find yourself feeling more happy and confident too?

Let's be real – it's hard to feel like an empowered and confident woman when you have holes in your underpants!

Dress up! Wear something you love – something that makes you happy. If that means sparkles and feathers, go for it! If it means something more stylishly simple like your favourite jeans and t-shirt, lean in to that too.

In my early sober days, sometimes I invested in a new dress to give me that little boost I needed to get me through the door. Other times I wore my favourite earrings or lipstick.

If it's a long event you're headed to, above all, make sure you're *comfortable*.

I've been to multiple 9-hour weddings and 5-hour parties over the past few years, which are a very different experience when you're sober! Sky-high heels were never a problem when I was drinking. *Time sped up; booze numbed the pain.* But sober? Not so much!

Remember: you want to have **fun**, first and foremost, so wear things that don't pinch or hurt - things that are *kind* to your body, and you'll enjoy the event that much more.

DRESS FOR SUCCESS

Which items in your wardrobe always make you feel amazing? Maybe you have a pair of comfy shoes you love, or a favourite perfume. Perhaps you have a dress that always feels kind to your body (in that it's both comfy and cute), or a bold new lipstick colour you're excited to try.

Plan (or draw!) a few ideas for your favourite outfits here:

LUCK, BE A LADY TONIGHT

In early sobriety, I bought a silver bracelet that I wore constantly.

Engraved inside (on the part that no-one else could see, but I knew was there) were the words: 'Stay here'.

I attended a ton of events in those first few weeks, and I wore the bracelet to every single one.

Just seeing the bracelet on my wrist somehow cut through all the turmoil in my head that spouted nonsense like: *"Just have one! What's the big deal?"*

It acted as a *symbol*, reminding me of all the reasons I wanted to remain alcohol-free: to experience a deeper, more honest relationship with my love, to pour my heart and soul into my creative endeavours, and to experience more freedom and joy in life.

It reminded me to 'stay here', on the scary but *oh-so*-rewarding sober side.

Because, let's face it, sobriety is not for the faint of heart. It takes courage, strength, and tenacity. It's a bold act of rebellion in a society that celebrates alcohol; a commitment to growth and evolution, and all the incredible magic and beauty wrapped up in that.

Carrying an object you believe is lucky, or that acts as a symbol, can boost your confidence and make you that much more likely to succeed.

TALISMAN MAGIC

Do you have a lucky charm?

If so, what do you love about it? Why is it meaningful to you and what does it symbolise, especially in regards to your sobriety?

How could you bring or wear your lucky charm to your next event?

Is it wearable? Could you incorporate it into your outfit somehow? Could you fit it into your purse? Or would you prefer to take a snapshot of your special talisman and carry that photo with you instead?

YOUR LUCKY CHARM

If you don't yet have a lucky charm, what object would feel meaningful for you?

What could you use as a symbol of your deepest intentions? The sky's the limit here! There are no rules; it's totally up to you. Any item you like can be *your* special talisman. Brainstorm a few ideas.

_____

_____

_____

_____

_____

How could you bring or wear your lucky charm to your next event to give you strength and boost your confidence?

Could it be incorporated into your outfit somehow? Will it fit into your bag? What's your plan, lucky duck?

_____

_____

_____

_____

_____

_____

AROMATIC ANCHORING

Aromatherapy is a holistic healing treatment utilising essential oils extracted from plants and herbs. Used throughout history for their therapeutic and healing benefits, these oils can help to support emotional balance, a sense of calm, and feelings of wellbeing.

Basically, they're powerful little gifts from nature! Best of all? They make amazing sober treats.

In early sobriety, I'd often put a drop or two in my bathtub for a luxurious soak, or dab a little lavender oil onto my pillow to help with sleep.

Most fascinating for us on this sobriety expedition is the concept of *Aromatic Anchoring*.

Located in the centre of the brain, the limbic system is believed to connect the mind to body, bridging the gap between psychological and physiological experiences.

Our sense of smell is the only sense directly linked to the limbic system. From the time we're born, smells and emotion are stored in this centre as one memory, which explains why aroma is so powerful at evoking snapshots in time.

For example, you walk past a store and smell apple pies baking, only to be instantly transported back to a memory of baking with your grandmother. Or you find yourself feeling curiously uneasy when you smell a certain cologne, because subconsciously it reminds you of an unhappy time or relationship.

The response is instant, and so are the effects on the brain's mental and emotional responses and our body chemistry.

SWEET SURRENDER

Which means we can harness this power for good!

Aromatic Anchoring is the idea of linking a smell to a desired feeling.

In my first few weeks socialising sober, meditating on an emotion I wanted to feel, I'd use an essential oil to become grounded to that emotion. Then I'd take the oil with me to each event, often wearing it as perfume!

The powerful thing about this, is that any time you feel fearful or resentful at an event, simply smelling the oil on your skin can bring you back to the emotion you *really* want to feel.

It's a secret little weapon you can take with you anywhere to make you feel safe.

Try it with me now!

Choose your favourite essential oil, or feel free to create your very own signature blend. Spend a few minutes doing a heart-filled meditation or visualisation while smelling your chosen oil.

You can use an oil diffuser to fill the room with the blissful scent, or simply place a drop between your hands, rub together, and breathe deeply three times.

Then carry the oil with you in your bag, or wear it as perfume. Return to it whenever you feel scared, overwhelmed, or resentful. Let it boost your confidence and guide you back to the emotions you *really* want to feel.

SCENT WITH LOVE

Sandalwood oil is said to be wonderful at soothing anxiety, while lemon oil boasts mood lifting properties.

Which are your favourite essential oils?

Have you tried making a signature blend by combining multiple essential oils in an oil diffuser?

If so, what are your favourite combinations?

ANCHOR IN

Going back to the emotions you want to feel (the moods and intentions we explored in Part 3), which oil and scent would you like to use to anchor you to each one?

Emotion:
_____
_____
_____

Oil:
_____
_____
_____

Emotion:
_____
_____
_____

Oil:
_____
_____
_____

INTROVERSION IS MY SUPERPOWER

If you haven't yet seen Author Amy Cuddy's TED Talk, *"Your Body Language Shapes Who You Are"*, it's well worth a watch! A Harvard professor and social psychologist, Amy's talk has been viewed tens of millions of times.

Her research shows that the simple act of adopting expansive poses (just like Wonder Woman or Superman!) can make us feel more powerful, confident, and assertive.

That is, our emotions take cues from our bodies.

Which means the next time we need to do a scary thing (like head to a big event sober, have a difficult conversation, or present to a group), we can use our bodies to help us feel more present and empowered.

Feeling nervous about that upcoming party? **Strike a power pose!** Stick your chest out, chin up, place your hands on your hips, and stand with your legs shoulder-width apart.

Hold the pose for two minutes, then walk through the door and watch your confidence skyrocket.

TRY IT WITH ME!

First up, how are your emotions and energy levels right now?

We're so close! You're about to head into an event as a non-drinker (possibly for the very first time!). How does it feel?

NOW, STRIKE A POWER POSE AND HOLD IT FOR TWO MINUTES.

Afterwards, how do you feel?

Did posing in this way help to change your thoughts and energy? In what way?

_____
_____
_____
_____
_____
_____
_____
_____
_____
_____
_____

Are there any other body movements or poses that work really well for you?

Try a couple now, before we head out the door!

Part 6:

Peer Pressure

"Because, despite what my teenage self believed, true confidence doesn't come from a bottle, or from the approval of others.

It comes from doing one brave thing after another and ==proving to yourself that you are capable of so much more than you ever believed possible.==

Because you are. We all are. So. Much. More."

– *Chameleon: Confessions of a Former People-Pleaser*

FITTING OUT

When you stop to think about it, isn't it pretty wild that we still feel peer pressure past the age of sixteen?

How many things do we do just to try to fit in?

When I first embarked on my sobriety path, this was one thing that scared me witless.

What would people say? *Would I still be invited anywhere? How on earth would I socialise without a drink in my hand?*

The times I was closest to giving up my hard-won sober status were the times I saw groups of friends on Facebook going to big, boozy events together.

I really didn't want to drink, but apparently I still desperately wanted to fit in. I was willing to trade what I truly wanted (to live my life authentically and alcohol-free), simply to be the same as everyone else.

I know I'm not alone in this. I hear from countless beautiful souls who worry about how they'll continue to fit in with their current friendship circles when they stop drinking. Each message is filled with fear; each person more terrified than the last of being the odd one out.

And it makes sense. **As humans, we crave connection. We long to belong.**

WHISTLE YOUR OWN TUNE

We fool ourselves into believing we enjoy being radical individuals, when in actual fact, we're often crippled by worries of what other people think; of being different, or of somehow standing out.

It's a fear well worth exploring within ourselves, because if we're afraid of being different, we can be brilliantly adept at finding ways to sabotage ourselves and our intentions.

We might 'accidentally' and expertly trip ourselves up so we can remain 'safe' in our current network of friends, family and peers.

But, here's the thing. **You don't have to abandon yourself in order to receive love from others.**

"But everyone else is doing it!" isn't a good enough reason to sacrifice yourself or betray your intentions.

You can spend the rest of your life trying to be like everyone else, or you can spend it being true to yourself.

Who wants to fit in, anyway? You're an adult now and the CEO of your own life. Why not actively choose to fit out? Rebel against the norm. Celebrate the myriad of ways you're different.

You don't have to give in to fit in.

You are enough, just as you are.

WHAT WILL PEOPLE THINK?!

Often, simply exploring this topic can help us to feel more confident.

What are some of your biggest fears around what people will think (or say) about you not drinking?

06 SOCIAL NORMS

Have there been times in the past when you didn't really feel like drinking, but did it anyway, just to fit in?

How did it feel?

_____
_____
_____
_____
_____
_____
_____
_____
_____
_____
_____
_____
_____
_____
_____

REBEL YELL

If you didn't care about fitting in, what are some of the things you always wished you could do?

If not now, when?

06 OWNING IT!

Cast your mind back to a time when you offered a friend a slice of cake or a cookie. If you reflect hard enough, you can probably recall a few different instances, with a few different friends or family members.

Think about how your friend responded. Did she laugh nervously and then say something like:

"Oh no, I really shouldn't."
"Ohhh, I wish I could but I *can't*. I'm on a diet." *(sad face)*.
"Don't tempt me!"

If so, what did you make of it? Did you feel like she *really* didn't want the dessert being offered? Or did it seem like she really *did* want it, but was forcing herself not to (in other words: suffering via deprivation and punishment)?

What was your reaction? Did you push the cookies even harder because you wanted to end her suffering?

If so, you're not alone. **When we see someone we care about struggling with an internal dilemma, it's natural to want to help end their heartache.**

UNMISTAKEABLE BELIEF

Now think about a time when a friend laughed and shook her head, or confidently said something like:

"No thanks."
"Not today."
"Not for me. I'm actually on a health kick, and I feel fantastic!"
"I don't feel like it today."

The funny and ironic thing about fear of judgement is that we tend to encounter less of it, the more we show **unshakeable confidence in our own choice.**

When *you* are happy with your decision, your confident, joyful energy is so reassuring to other people. They trust that you know what you're doing, simply because you're so confident in your choice. Which means they're less likely to try to pressure you, or convince you to change your mind!

Whenever I felt myself being triggered by someone else's choices or behaviour, I always loved to repeat the mantra: "I choose happiness. I choose sobriety. I'm doing this for *me*."

Just like choosing your attitude and frame of mind, this affirmation is such a great way to remember **this is *your* journey; everyone else is on their own path.**

06 AFFIRMATIVE!

A tactic that can really help with this, is to switch your comments from something negative to something affirmative and positive. So, rather than talking about what you *can't* (or don't want to) do; talk about what you *can* do. For example:

Rather than: "I can't stay late."
Try: "I can stay until 9pm."

Rather than: "I can't drink tonight."
Try: "I'll have a mocktail / club soda / coconut juice."

You get the gist. **Play around with a few positive phrases below to help you fully own your choice:**

IT'S NOT ME, IT'S YOU.

Remember when you were drinking, how annoyed you were when you lost a drinking partner, or when friends or family members wouldn't drink with you?

The truth is, our abstinence can be a huge adjustment for others, too.

The mere fact that we're making changes in our lives may cause ripples in our relationships at first, which is completely normal and understandable.

One way to handle this is to be a shining example. It's entirely possible they may never have seen anyone happily living sober before. Show them just how fun sobriety can be!

Think of yourself as a trailblazer; a game-changer!

People who rarely drink will think nothing of your choice not to imbibe.

Those who struggle with their *own* relationship with alcohol, however, might be tempted to pressure you. In which case, it pays to remember: their reaction has so much more to do with *them*, than it does with *you*.

Don't take it personally. Have compassion for where they're at in their life, and keep moving forward.

MEMORY LANE

Can you think of a time in the past when you were triggered by a friend choosing not to drink with you? Maybe they weren't feeling the best, or had an early meeting.

What was your reaction?

Were you totally cool about it, or did you have some strong words to say?

_____

_____

_____

_____

_____

_____

_____

_____

_____

_____

_____

_____

WHAT WAS IT *REALLY* ABOUT?

Was your reaction about the other person, or was it really about you?

Be honest; there's zero judgement here. Whenever a work friend told me she could only have one drink because she had an early meeting, my reaction was something along the lines of: *"WHAT? Unacceptable! You have to drink with me!"*. In other words: I didn't care about her meeting; I cared about having a drinking partner!

06 IT'S NOT PERSONAL

How does this perspective change the way you take other people's reactions on board?

Does it allow you to have more compassion for where they're at in their own life's journey, and free you from taking it personally?

_____

_____

_____

_____

_____

_____

_____

_____

_____

_____

_____

_____

_____

_____

"Some people might push your buttons just to test your resolve, or get emotional when you stand up for yourself. That's entirely their choice, but here's what you need to remember: it doesn't have anything to do with you. Their reactions are not your responsibility. ==You don't owe anyone an apology for taking care of yourself.=="

– Chameleon: Confessions of a Former People-Pleaser

FUNNY BONE

Maintaining your sense of humour is one delicious technique that can help relieve the tension.

One of my favourite mantras (especially when heading into an event I'm nervous about, or fear I might be peer pressured) is:

"This event will either be fun, or funny."

I simply make up my mind to view it as one of those two things - *and it works!*

For example:

Everyone accepts that I'm drinking sparkling apple juice, and we end up having a whale of a time? = Fun!

Sally-Anne makes a big, dramatic scene about the fact that I'm not drinking alcohol? = Funny!

Okay, I'll admit, perhaps it doesn't always feel all that amusing in the moment, but if it helps, imagine telling the animated version of the event to your best friend the next day.

Now (in the grand scheme of things), it seems kinda' funny (in a ridiculous kind of way), right?

AMUSEMENT PARK

Think about the last event you went to. What are some aspects of the occasion you could choose to view through this lens?

Conversations or parts of the night I could view as fun, light-hearted, merry or jolly:

Conversations or parts of the night I could view as funny, amusing, entertaining, or silly:

06 BRASS TACKS

The thing about other people's reactions, is that underlying their behaviour is the much bigger issue of *fear of judgement*.

You see, not only are we terrified we'll be judged for not drinking, but it's possible other people are also scared that our decision not to drink is a judgement of *them* and *their* life choices.

Easing this undercurrent of conflict and fear comes down to clear communication.

Sit your friend down for a heart-to-heart and reassure them that *you* wanting to do something for your own health and wellbeing is by no means a judgement of them or their choices. Practice open, loving communication. Speak up, tell the truth, and ask for what you need. Explain that all you want from them is their love and support, while offering them the same.

Then, if it feels good, why not invite them to share more about their feelings, or even better, to join you? Staying focused on the positives can help to diffuse any stress.

You could say something like: "I'm actually excited to experience life without alcohol for a while. Do you find that thought scary? Why is that?"

Or: "This is just a little health experiment I want to do to see if I sleep/think/eat/move/breathe better. Why don't you join me? It'll be fun!"

Throughout history, pioneers, leaders and visionaries were often mocked, before everyone finally realised they were actually on to something!

HEY THERE, TRENDSETTER!

The beautiful thing about being an innovator is that you light the way for others to follow in your footsteps. My own sobriety path was illuminated by the courageous souls who went before me and shared their story. *You* can be that same light for somebody else.

As it turns out, many people actually want to stop drinking; they just aren't sure how to go about it.

At your upcoming event, if someone shows genuine interest in your sobriety and the benefits you've experienced so far, what will you tell them? How will you invite them to join you?

06 SAYING NO

If all else fails, remember that "NO" is a complete sentence.

This concept was an utter revelation to my people-pleasing mind just a few years ago, but it's true. 'No' really is a complete sentence.

So are:
"No, thanks."
"Not tonight."
"I'm driving."
"I've got plans in the morning."
"I don't feel like it."
"I'm on a health kick."
"I feel better without it."
"I don't drink."

If you're feeling nervous about what to say to people, remember that it's completely up to you how much you want to share about your decision not to drink.

It's not your responsibility to make others feel comfortable. You don't owe anyone an explanation, any more than you owe anyone an explanation about why you choose not to smoke, or to consume any other drug or toxic substance.

It's perfectly fine to choose what's best for you, even if it swims firmly against the mainstream.

Your decision is yours alone, and 'NO' truly is a complete sentence.

GIDDY UP

Okay, let's practice! Take a deep breath and try out some scripts below. It truly does get so much easier with repetition.

"Hi, hon! Let me get you a drink."

What will you say in this situation?

_____
_____
_____
_____
_____
_____
_____
_____
_____
_____
_____
_____
_____
_____

06 FOR REAL?

"What do you mean you want soda water? Aren't you drinking tonight? Why not? For how long?"

What will you say in this situation?

JUST ONE SIP!

"Ooh, you have to taste this drink - it's so good!"

What will you say in this situation?

_____
_____
_____
_____
_____
_____
_____
_____
_____
_____
_____
_____
_____
_____
_____

06 COME ON!

"But it's my BIRTHDAY! You have to drink with me!"

What will you say in this situation?

_____
_____
_____
_____
_____
_____
_____
_____
_____
_____
_____
_____
_____
_____

Above all, **don't let this role-playing freak you out.** Just as we covered when ordering drinks, the more you practice and have fun with it, the easier it'll be. Pinky swear!

A NEW DAWN

Last but not least, extend people forgiveness if and when they get it wrong. Because they will. It's inevitable.

We're all highly complicated, emotional beings constantly making mistakes and (hopefully!) learning from them.

I remember when I was drinking, and I'd see strong, sober women out and about. Women who were sexy, articulate, and who had the good sense to leave the bar before things got messy.

"Boring!", I'd declare to anyone who'd listen, often splashing the drink out of my glass as I waved it in the woman's general direction.

Meanwhile, on the inside, I had quiet respect for them. Secretly, I'd wonder: *How does she do that? How does she have the confidence and self-assurance to shrug off peer pressure and make healthy choices for herself?*

Lead with compassion.

Give it time and patience, and give people the benefit of the doubt. They might get it wrong today, but tomorrow might just be a whole new ball game.

People can change, just like you.

Part 7:

Rocking the Event

"I thought about all the times I'd been drunk, and how it had made me feel like I was the most powerful seductress in the history of the Universe. In reality, no doubt I'd looked like a drunken buffoon. Sobriety – being completely conscious – really *was* sexy."

– *A Happier Hour*

SOBER IS SEXY

Ok, hot stuff. Here we go...

We're about to head into the event *(cue excited/nervous/terrified squeals!).*

Before we go, give your body a little shimmy, shake out your hair, and rewrite that worn out old 'boring teetotaller' stereotype.

The glorious thing about sobriety is that it invites us to step into bona fide confidence and empowerment - and what could be more liberating and attractive than that?

Sobriety really *is* sexy.

As is:

- Becoming more of who you truly are.
- Enjoying yourself, without relying on a toxic substance to bring the party energy.
- Feeling like a rockstar because you didn't do something cringe-worthy at a work function.
- Not saying something you immediately regret and can never take back.
- Not drunk dialling your ex.
- Getting home safely.
- Waking up with your phone, keys, purse, dignity - and most of all, *memory* - completely intact.

WHAT WOULD YOU ADD?

What's the sexiest part of sobriety for you?

Have fun with this part, exploring both the positives of sobriety (all the things you get to enjoy sober) and the negatives of drinking (all the things you get to avoid tonight!).

CHOOSING YOUR ENERGY

Look, if you usually socialise over a few drinks, it's completely normal to feel nervous about attending events without a drink in your hand. I know it can be *oh-so*-tempting to stay home and hide for the rest of your life, but the truth is, we often learn best by jumping in the deep end and strengthening our muscles (reinforcing the lessons) through repetition.

One aspect of drinking that was incredibly seductive to me was having the chance to let off steam. One night, as I was getting ready for a friend's party, I found myself wishing I could just cut *loose* at this jamboree, like I did when I was drinking.

Suddenly it occurred to me: *What the heck was I on about?* Of course *I could still run amuck like I used to!*

I simply had to make the decision to.

I went into that party with that same excited energy I used to have in my drinking years. I really let my hair down, and laughed and danced - all while drinking alcohol-free mocktails - and *BAM!* That energy was so attractive to people. It was magnetic. As different friends grabbed me to chat, I realised I was having an absolute blast!

This is the power of choosing your energy.

SET YOUR SIGHTS

Another time, only three weeks into my sobriety, a bunch of my favourite ex-colleagues invited me to meet them for drinks at a trendy inner-city bar.

I really wanted to go. I missed them. But I'd be lying if I said I felt confident about the whole thing. The old me would have been counting down the minutes until it started. The new me was worried. Everyone had always known me as the girl with the champagne glass in her hand.

If I wasn't that person anymore, *who would I be?*

And then I remembered: the night wasn't about alcohol. It was about spending time with people I genuinely cared about.

Start by shifting your thoughts.

Focus on all the good things about the party that don't involve alcohol: the beautiful venue, the delicious food, fun with friends, having the chance to dress up.

Before long, you might just find yourself howling with laughter and forgetting all about your self-consciousness (I certainly did).

This is what awaits you when you choose to focus on the bigger picture. Whether it's the chance to have fun and be silly, spend time with your favourite people, or enjoy being in beautiful surroundings, socialising really *is* about so much more than drinking.

FOCUS ON THE GOOD STUFF

Remember: having the right mindset can move mountains. Go into your events expecting to have fun! Focus on all the good things about the party that don't involve alcohol.

What are you most looking forward to at this event?

CALL IN THE REINFORCEMENTS

How are you directing your mind to focus on what's really important?

Are you just going to *decide* that this event is about having fun with your friends and letting your hair down, alcohol-free style? Which of your sober tools will you use to reinforce your intentions? Will you use visualisation, reviewing your lists, giving yourself a little treat or bravery reward, or another one of the other strategies we've covered so far? Brainstorm here:

POWER THROUGH THE AWKWARDNESS

"It's always awkward before it's elegant."

Gosh, I love this quote. I first heard it from Gina DeVee in regards to doing things in business for the first time, but it helped me so much in early sobriety.

It was one of my favourite mantras in my first few weeks (and months!) of learning to live alcohol-free. It helped me to take the pressure off myself and feel like my utter weirdness about how to behave in public and social events as a non-drinker, was all just a normal part of the process.

Really, it's a shame that we think we have to turn to alcohol to save us from that awkward half hour at the start of an event. Because you know what? Nobody ever died of awkward.

Once you get through those precarious few minutes, the deeper, more fun and real conversations tend to follow.

Better yet, as you grow accustomed to not drinking, the awkwardness begins to fade away. Before you know it, you'll be the proud owner of a fabulous new soberpower: feeling comfortable in social situations without alcohol. *Yes please!*

07 CRUNCH THE NUMBERS

If you think about how many minutes out of each event were actually cringey, you may also realise they encompass only a very small part of the night.

When you head into your next event, take a moment to check the clock during the most awkward parts. Record the numbers. **How many minutes in total did those tricky spells take up? How many minutes were *not* cringey?**

And for bonus points: what percentage of time at the event was actually uncomfortable? For example, 30 *cringe-fest* minutes divided by 240 total event minutes = only 12.5%. Which means 87.5% of the event *wasn't* awkward. Sounds like pretty good odds, no?

THE CURIOSITY GAME

About seven months into my sobriety, I met up with a bunch of friends at a fancy, inner-city hotel for a high tea afternoon.

Despite my resolve and everything I'd learnt in the months prior, in the weeks leading up to this date, I was nervous. This wasn't just a 'cake and scones' high tea; this event included champagne.

I'd already rehearsed asking for sparkling water with lemon, but I was worried about how it would feel to be out with my friends again and be the only one not drinking. Back when we'd hit the town every Friday night, I'd always planned elaborate agendas, devised to keep them out drinking with me as late as possible. On this day, they'd be seeing a very different Bex.

Would they beg me to drink with them, telling me this sobriety thing had gone far enough? Would they think I was completely boring? Would they have a ton of drunken shenanigans to talk about, while I felt dull and left out?

Ohhh, The Beast (or the Wine Witch!) had a field day in my mind, reinforcing every fear that popped into it.

INQUIRING MINDS

And yet, when the day finally arrived, I *remembered*...

This day wasn't about which liquid was in my glass; it was about *reconnecting* with my favourite people. Deciding to focus on *them* helped me to feel less self-conscious, which helped immensely with settling pre-event jitters!

As I did my hair and make-up and chose which outfit to wear, I was surprised and delighted to find my nerves had all but disappeared. I felt only butterflies of excitement. I couldn't wait to squeeze them all and find out what they'd been up to.

With this frame of mind, I skipped into that event, and hugged the bananas out of them. The hours flew by. The food was delicious, and the stories were so plentiful and hilarious that I found myself frequently crying with laughter. It turned out to be a beautiful afternoon of catching up.

Get curious.

If, at any time, you're feeling nervous about an event, take the pressure and focal point off yourself. Turn your attention to discovering what everyone *else* has been up to since you last saw them.

Trust me, once you ask a question or two, no-one will even notice (or care!) that you're not drinking alcohol. *Hurray!*

SHERLOCK HOLMES

Heading to a large work function or networking event where you don't really know anyone? *Great!* This strategy works even better. As you meet new people, play the Detective. **Make it a little game to find out at least three new things about each person.**

Stumped about what to ask? Have fun with it! You could ask them questions like:

- What's your biggest goal for the next 12 months?
- What's a class you've always wanted to take?
- Which place have you always wanted to visit?
- What did you always want to be when you were little?
- Have you ever daydreamed about changing your first name? To what?
- Have you ever met one of your heroes?
- Have you ever set two friends up on a date? (How'd it go?)
- Have you ever won an award or trophy? What was it for?

You get the picture.

Ask anything you're curious about. Go deep. **Often we experience social anxiety because we can't stand small talk.** Become engaged in people's answers and stories. You'll learn more about them and get rock-solid practice at socialising sober.

You might surprise yourself and actually have fun! And if not, remind yourself you don't have to be the last one to leave - you can leave as soon as you want to. You can even drive home!

07
FOLLOW THE CLUES

Who are you expecting to see at your upcoming event?

Do you know who else has RSVP'd? Which of your friends or colleagues are going? Which new people might be there?

SCINTILLATING DIALOGUE

What are some topics you could chat about?

If you're expecting to see friends or colleagues you haven't seen in a while, what are some topics of conversation you could bring up? For example their recent travels, career changes, or home renovations, etc?

CHILD-LIKE CURIOSITY

What could you ask each new person?

If you're expecting to meet new people at the event, choosing (and practicing!) three solid questions before you go can help to make them easier to remember. What are three questions you like the sound of?

Here are some more ideas to get you started:

- What was your very first job?
- What was your worst haircut of all time?
- What's something you've tried and will never, ever try again?
- What's the best cake you've ever eaten?
- What's the worst piece of advice you've ever been given?
- Where and when do you get your best ideas?

_____

_____

_____

_____

_____

_____

_____

_____

DON'T STOP NOW!

The more these questions roll off your tongue, the easier and more enjoyable your night will be. **What other questions could you ask?**

_____
_____
_____
_____
_____
_____
_____
_____
_____
_____
_____
_____
_____
_____

Great! Got those prompts fresh in your mind? **Now, go rock that party!** It's time. Make yourself proud. You're ready, and you've got this.

Part 8:
Looking Ahead

"What if everything I ever believed about my idea of fun, was wrong? Could it be that I got so drunk at events because I wasn't comfortable there in the first place?"

– *A Happier Hour*

MORNING-AFTER REFLECTION

You're back! You did it! You made it through an event sober. I'm so proud of you!

Knowing that socialising sober is a skill we can get better at, reviewing our progress can help us to recognise our strengths and better prepare for the *next* event. So let's review our lab notes…

How did you feel before this event?

How were your emotions? Did you feel nervous; excited; hopeful? What were your biggest fears or anxieties, going in?

_____

_____

_____

_____

_____

_____

_____

_____

_____

_____

08 ELECTRIC ENERGY

What did you prepare to make this event more fun or easier?

Thinking back over everything we've covered (especially the aspects we dove into in *Part 2: Prep like a Sober Rockstar!*), how did you boost your happy vibes and prepare yourself and your environment for success?

CELEBRATE YOUR SUCCESS

What went right at this event?

Which parts were the most fun or meaningful to you? Which parts went better than you'd hoped?

MASTER STRATEGIST

Which socialising-sober strategies worked best for you?

Was it instigating mindset shifts and retraining your brain (like we covered in Part 3)? Was it practicing all the confidence hacks we covered in Part 5? Or was it the Curiosity Game we covered in Part 7? Which strategies were your favourites?

_____
_____
_____
_____
_____
_____
_____
_____
_____
_____
_____
_____
_____
_____
_____

SURPRISE AND DELIGHT

Which actions did you take that you're most proud of?

How did you surprise yourself at this event? Which actions felt scary at first, but have given you confidence that you can actually get better at this socialising sober thing?

_____

_____

_____

_____

_____

_____

_____

_____

_____

_____

_____

_____

_____

_____

08 LET'S HONE THOSE SKILLS!

OK, now over to the parts you'd love to improve.

Which part of the event did you find the most challenging?
Which moments felt particularly awkward, or tough?

BABY STEPS

Was there a socialising-sober strategy that you forgot this time, or would like to improve in some way?

It's tough to remember every single tip and trick the first time around. Which techniques would you like to improve or incorporate next time?

STRENGTHENING OUR SKILLSET

What lessons did you learn that could help you next time?

It's true; every single event can teach us something. What did this occasion teach you?

BRING IT HOME!

What are you excited to try differently for your next event?

Dream bigger and better, baby! Whether it's your outfit choice, a different reframe, or a new phrase you can't wait to try out, what are you pumped to try next time?

08 BUMPS IN THE ROAD

I have to admit, there was one event a couple of years into my sobriety that didn't go *all* that smoothly...

It was a weekend affair. Dom and I arrived at the hotel on Thursday night for the networking portion.

I'd never been a big fan of networking events, not even when I was drinking. The small talk about what you did, how long you'd done it for, and which department you did it in, always drove me bonkers. I'd always avoided them as much as possible, regardless of whether free drinks had been involved.

But I was excited about this one.

Dom and I were finalists for a prestigious Australian business award, and I couldn't wait to meet the other biz owners and share our story and message.

Of course, when I look back now, I can see the danger signs. Despite my enthusiasm, I was also exhausted from a hectic week, hungry, and wearing painful heels. The only alcohol-free options were Coke or plain water *(ugh)*.

When it came time to give my speech, I got flustered and messed it up. Afterwards, during chit-chat, I couldn't seem to shake my awkwardness or nerves.

It was just the perfect storm of a difficult night, really. Not the end of the world, by any means, but walking back to our hotel room, I couldn't help but feel deflated. I felt sad that it was sometimes hard.

In that moment... honestly? I felt triggered.

TUNNEL LIGHT

Back in our room, we discovered a complimentary bottle of chilled champagne had been placed on our table. And I could only shake my head and laugh.

"That's it!" I declared to Dom, heading straight for the mini bar.

Pushing past the ridiculous number of booze bottles, I reached way in the back for the dark chocolates. I kicked off my shoes, made us both a cup of tea, and jumped onto the bed, savouring each delicious bite of those peppermint chocolates as I slowed my breathing.

Aahhh, soooo much better.

The next morning, of course, I felt human again. Later that evening, as I applied my makeup for the gala dinner, I was so grateful to be feeling nerves and excitement, rather than numbing myself.

This time, there was delicious food, sparkling mineral water with fresh lime (my favourite!), and a ton of inspiration from the guest speakers.

The whole night felt magical. *And I didn't miss alcohol even one tiny bit.*

Sometimes days (or events or conversations) will be hard. But the next one just might exceed your expectations.

Bad days are just bad days.

Hold on for the good ones. They're coming for you, and you'll be *so* glad you waited for them.

08 ROSE COLOURED

Can you think of a time when you were drinking and the event *still* wasn't all that much fun?

The same is true of experiencing events sober.

It's the unique, magical combination of energy, mood, people, atmosphere and entertainment that makes an event pleasurable - not what's in your glass.

As you recap on your first foray into socialising sober, be kind to yourself. Be patient. The early phase of sobriety can be tough; I feel you. I promise it does get so much better – with time and experience.

The next time you crave a drink, think about what it is you're really hoping alcohol will do for you. Speed up time? Make the event more fun?

Alcohol really doesn't have that ability, as much as we might have once believed it did.

Perhaps you're hoping drinking will make you one of the gang? Or bring you closer to people?

Newsflash! Alcohol doesn't equal connection.

You will be just as good a friend, if not infinitely better, if you remove alcohol from your life. This new life chapter presents the perfect opportunity to build friendships that are based on more than just sharing a bottle.

METAMORPHOSIS

Now that you've done a little hobnobbing alcohol-free, it's worth taking a pause to explore how much you've *changed*.

It's funny how attached we can be to our old ideas and identities. There can be so much temptation to cling to the old – to reminisce and romanticise things that no longer serve us – rather than embrace the new.

For so long after I stopped drinking, I kept trying to fit myself into my old life and identity. When friends invited me to big, boozy affairs, I told myself I had to go, and dreaded every second leading up to it.

Over time, I started saying a loving 'no, thank you' to events that didn't make my heart giddy with excitement.

In turn, this created more space and energy for me to attend events where I met kindred spirits, shared deep conversations, and howled with laughter. And later, driving home from these events, I felt completely filled up.

It's okay to change. We were always meant to.

If there's one thing that's true about sobriety, it's that we grow and evolve at lightning-quick pace.

Minds change. Hearts open. Quantum leaps take place.

As Cheryl Strayed put it so brilliantly: "Don't surrender all your joy for an idea you used to have about yourself that isn't true anymore."

SOBER BUTTERFLY

What have you learnt about yourself this far into your sobriety quest, about who you really are, and the types of activities you enjoy?

Are you more introverted than you expected? Do you prefer big events or quiet, intimate hang-outs? Do you like to socialise at parties, over dinner, or while grabbing a smoothie?

REDEFINING FUN

For years, I believed I could only have fun if alcohol was involved. It broke my heart to say goodbye to drinking because I truly believed I'd never have - or *BE* - fun, *ever again*.

Turns out it was just my definition of fun that was out of whack. Because, as you and I know, there's absolutely nothing fun about hangovers, shame, or regret.

One of the most beautiful things about about sobriety is that it offers us the chance to experiment and explore. To get to know ourselves again and find out what makes us happy.

I once read an article that stated: 'What do you do for fun?' is a question that most adults find difficult to answer.

Is it any wonder then, that we put booze on a pedestal as the one and only magic key to 'fun'?

Never mind all the heartache and drama that comes with drinking - if we don't know any other way to play, we give our power away to alcohol.

As you change, it's completely normal (and healthy) to redefine fun. You may find you don't particularly want to keep going to the same places and expecting different results. For many people, this means avoiding bars and clubs or hanging out in other places that no longer feel good.

08 TASTES CHANGE

Are there any places or events you don't find fun anymore?

Is there a particular type of venue or party that no longer feels good? Do you suspect that perhaps the reason you got drunk at particular events was because you weren't comfortable there in the first place? If so, what kind of events in particular?

SHAKE UP THE SCENE

You see, we can't expect to just remove alcohol and magically have a life we love. Putting down the glass is just one part of it.

A vast amount of time opens up for us in sobriety. Time we can use to follow our passions and explore new ways to socialise.

Why not get creative and have some fun with it!

Rather than meeting friends at the pub or a party where the only 'entertainment' is drinking, make plans to meet for a scrumptious brunch at a cafe with a view, or organise a fun daytime activity you can do together, like playing a round of mini golf, taking a ceramics class, or heading off on a day trip.

Maybe you love to paint, sing in a choir, or go for early morning hikes through the hills. Or perhaps you fancy the idea of booking cinema or theatre tickets, or hosting a pot-luck, home movie night.

Embrace the chance to socialise with people on a deeper level, and in a whole new way. Dream up new activities that promote connection; adventures that bond you through sharing old memories and creating new ones.

What a great way to reframe our old notions of 'socialising', right? How empowering to be able to embrace our newly-discovered selves, and create the type of social life that fills us with joy.

NOVEL EXPERIENCES

Maybe your social calendar used to be filled with big, fancy events and high-pressure dinner parties. So what? The great news is you don't have to do the same old things if your heart is calling you to embrace something new.

The problem with drinking for so long, is we can forget what on earth we even used to *enjoy* before wine came along. Have a brainstorm now. From museums and art galleries, to camping and beach picnics.

What are some ways you'd like to socialise differently in future?

_____

_____

_____

_____

_____

_____

_____

_____

_____

_____

NEIGHBOURHOOD VIBE

Are there any cool events coming up in your local area?

If so, which ones feel fun and exciting for you? Are there any groups you might like to join, or places you might like to visit? What activities or classes have you always wanted to try? Jot down a few ideas here:

Now, pick one event or activity you'll invite a friend to this week. Then grab your phone and make it happen! **Say hello to a whole new social life you actually love!**

Final Love Note

Congratulations, you incredible lightbeam!

You now have a plethora of tools, tips and resources to help you create the kind of social life that allows you to be more of who you truly are, and fills you with joy!

Here's to Your *Growth*.

In 2018, when I married my love and we organised our dream, alcohol-free wedding, I was so curious whenever anyone said: "Oh I can't dance / make a speech / chat to new people sober!"

It made me realise how *brave* we all are. You and me, doing all these things sober, all day long. Dancing; socialising; speaking up; telling the truth; asking for what we need.

Standing on our own two feet, day after day, without a lick of Dutch Courage.

The truth is, early sobriety often feels challenging because it *IS* freakin' challenging. Not just for you and me, but for *everyone* who has ever used alcohol as a crutch.

When I first stopped drinking, I often felt annoyed at how hard this felt. My inner teenager would pitch a fit for days about why *I* had to be the one to change, while others stayed cozy in their comfort zones.

Slowly, I realised I had it all wrong. I didn't *have* to change. I could easily choose to keep stubbornly plodding down the path I was on; a path that was making me increasingly unhappy.

Or I could think about how amazing it was that **I took the chance to change.** That my heart had requested more from life, and what an incredible gift that was in itself.

Because, here's the thing. Although it can feel scary and uncomfortable and painful at times, over the long term, it truly is *growth* that generates happiness.

Not staying stuck. Not being afraid to be different from our friends or family. Not consuming more drinks or food or clothes or electronics, or the myriad of other things our society tells us to consume in order to find happiness.

Not shrinking yourself to be the same person you were a year ago.

But, taking action. Solving problems. Overcoming new challenges. **Boldly going deeper into your relationships.**

What you're doing right now - choosing to up-end everything you've ever known in order to create a new, healthier life for yourself and everyone you care about - it's a true to testament to the courage and spirit that live within you.

Go ahead and grow, angel. Follow your heart. Reach your full potential.

Give yourself permission to change and evolve, and become anything and everything you've ever wanted to be.

You are limitless, brave, amazing, and so much stronger than you know. I wish you everything you dream of and more.

With love,
Bex

About the Author

Rebecca Weller is a Health and Life Coach, Bestselling Author, and Speaker. Named 'one of Perth's leading Healthpreneurs' by The Sunday Times Magazine, Rebecca helps women from around the world to get their sparkle back and create a life they love.

Author of the bestselling sobriety memoir, *A Happier Hour, Up All Day, Chameleon: Confessions of a Former People-Pleaser*, and many more, Rebecca writes about love, life, and the strength and potential of the human spirit.

Her work has been featured by The Telstra Business Awards, The Australian, The Huffington Post, MindBodyGreen, Fast Company, Good Health Magazine, Marie Claire Australia, and Elle Quebec.

Rebecca lives in sunny Perth, Western Australia, with her husband, Dominic.

Learn more, and receive a weekly love note full of inspiration, at: **BexWeller.com**.

Plus! Get your free monthly social calendar planning template and special bonus gifts at: **BexWeller.com/RSVP**.